I

LAKE DISTRICT

Dalesman

First published in Great Britain 2002 by
Dalesman Publishing Company Limited
Stable Courtyard, Broughton Hall
Skipton, North Yorkshire BD23 3AZ

© Dalesman Publishing Company Limited
Compiled by Paul Jackson

A British Cataloguing in Publication record
is available for this book

ISBN 1 85568 200 1

Cover origination by Grasmere Digital Imaging Limited
Printed by Amadeus Press, Cleckheaton, West Yorkshire

Also in this series:
THE LITTLE BOOK OF YORKSHIRE
ISBN 1 85568 194 3

INTRODUCTION

For centuries the Lake District has inspired poets, writers and artists and so it would be easy to fill a small book like this with romantic and poignant sayings by the famous who claim to have discovered their inner soul – or even paradise – in England's most glorious region.

However, that would be to miss out on

the gentle, sometimes ironic sense of humour needed by the ordinary Lakeland folk; those who have to earn a living despite a harsh landscape and predictably unpredictable weather but who nevertheless manage to raise a wry smile – even if it is often at the expense of the millions of sightseers and outdoor enthusiasts who descend on their territory for pleasure.

Here you will find a mixture of

immortal lines about the Lake District and its people from renowned poets, such as Wordsworth, and respected travel and guide writers like Wainwright to local wags and wily Cumbrian characters including the infamous Will Ritson.

If you can seen the Isle of Man then it's going to rain. If you can't see it – then it is raining.

West Coast saying

There's just one thing more beautiful than a nice Herdwick sheep… and that's a lady, nicely dressed.

Langdale farmer

Anyone who lives at the Lakes can hardly shake off Wordsworth. He haunts the place.

W G Collingwood, 1902

A dry season tourist once sought to
explore,
Where doth the water come down to
Lodore?
Quoth a Cumbrian maid with a toss of
her bonnet,
You may well seek Lodore, for you're
sitting upon it.
*Verse of unknown origin on the
disappearance of Lodore Falls during a dry
spell*

Oh Wasdale, where are thy charms,
 That poets have found in thy face;
Better dwell in the midst of alarms,
 Than stay in this watery place.
 Miss Knowles, 1869

Don't look at the hill and grumble –
climb it!
Old sign at Traveller's Rest, Kirkstone Pass

When the fire's on the hearth,
And good cheer abounds,
We'll drink to Joe Bowman,
And his Ullswater hounds,
For we ne'er shall forget
How he woke us at dawn.
With the crack of his whip
And the sound of his horn.

Song about 19th century huntsman Joe
Bowman of Lowther Vale

Good yal (ale), a mate, or being dry,
Or if you will be by-and-by,
Or any other reason why.
Cumbrian cure for teetotalism

Yan, tyan, tethera, methera, pimp,
sethera, lethera, hovera, dovera, dick.
*1 to 10 in the ancient sheep counting system
used around Borrowdale and Keswick*

The stranger, from the moment he sets foot upon these Sands, seems to leave the turmoil and traffic of the world behind him; and, crossing the majestic plain when the sea has retired, he beholds, rising apparently from its base, the cluster of mountains among which he is going to wander, and towards whose recesses, by the vale of Conistone, he is gradually and peacefully led.

Wordsworth (on Morecambe Sands)

Tak a walk on an empty stomach – it dizna matter whose.

Cumbrian cure for insomnia

When the wind gets going, you wonder how the house stands up. You can sometimes feel the pressure of air on your ears when you are in the sitting room.

Quote from former tenants of the Traveller's Rest, Kirkstone Pass

"What happens if the rope breaks?"
"Don't worry about that, we have plenty more ropes."
Response to concerned pupil on Lakes climbing course

Oh, mortal man that liv'st on bread
How come thy nose to be so red?
Thou silly ass, that looks so pale,
It is by drinking Birkett's Ale.
Sign at Mortal Man Inn, Troutbeck,
showing two men — one rosy and fat, the
other thin and miserable

There is an air of natural delight about the Cumbrian scenery that is unique. It is inimitable, like a child born under a lucky star; in feature, in complexion, in personal appeal it wins you. The hills have a natural tendency to make interesting shapes against the skyline.

Edmund Vale, North Country

Thence to Kendall, pure her state is,
Prudent too her magistrate is...
Here it likes me to be dwelling,
Boozing, loving, stories telling...
Richard Braithwaite, 17th century

If 't's fine, tak thar cwoat;
If 't's wet, please tha' sell.
Cumbrian advice

In Westmorland there were whole vallies of danes, all relations, and known, when they could get out of their native hollows, by their red heads, and their language being like the baaing of sheep.

A Walker, Tour from London to the Lakes, 1791

It has been noticed that in the Cumbrian dialects there are an excessive number of words for the actions of striking and beating. This may be due partly to the descent of the inhabitants from the pugnacious Vikings, and partly to the unsettled condition of the border counties in more modern days.

H S Cowper, 1899

Lakeland is not fashioned for motorists: cars can penetrate the interior in only a few places. It is largely a preserve of walkers. The most exhilarating and rewarding form of pedestrian travel is fell walking.

A Wainwright, master fell walker

Retreating and beating and meeting
and sheeting,
Delaying and staying and playing and
spraying,
Advancing and prancing and glancing
and dancing,
Recoiling, turmoiling and toiling and
boiling...
Robert Southey at Lodore Falls

Thou mun be lang in t' legs an' lank in guts afore thou canst follow t' hounds.

Will Ritson's assessment of a huntsman

We slept at Carlisle. I have not forgiven them for destroying their quiet old walls, and building two lumpy things like madhouses. The old gates had such a respectable appearance.

Sir Walter Scott, 1828

May God Almighty grant His aid
To Keswick and its woollen trade.
Old stone inscription

Surely there is no other place in this whole wonderful world quite like Lakeland....no other so exquisitely lovely, no other so charming, no other that calls so insistently across a gulf of distance. All who truly love Lakeland are exiles when away from it.

Alfred Wainwright's opening paragraph in his Pictorial Guide to the Lakeland Fells

She'd taak a banty cock into layan'
an egg.
Said of a woman who talks too much

Old Betty having dwelt here all her
days,
Can't understand the tourists' lavish
praise;
"Eh, dear," she cries, "Why mak seck
fuss and chatter,
"There's nowt to see but hills and trees
and watter."

*A Windermere local who on her 80th
birthday ventured for the first time to one of
the beauty spots, not a half-hour from her
home*

He wor a varra quiet auld man.
He'd nea pride aboot him an' varra lile
to say.
Will Ritson on Wordsworth

They're pluckin' geese i' Scotland an'
sending t' feathers here.
*Old Cumbrian saying when snow starts
to fall*

So richly blessed by Nature, Lakeland has not unworthily paid Nature back by giving to mankind the master poet of the hills, the dales, the little daisy, and the running stream.

Arthur Mee, 1930

Bulls cannot long be kept sane in these narrow valleys; the constantly repeated echoes of their own bellowings make them mad.

Mrs Linton on Borrowdale, 1860s

If I were a lover, and loved a lass
Who lived on top of Rossett Pass,
While I abode at Dungeon Ghyll,
I'd swear by all that's good or ill
To love and cherish her ever and ever
But nea visit her — never and never!
Traditional verse about the steep Rossett
Ghyll path

Rust-red are the mountains
and white fall the fountains
When over Helvellyn fly wintry gales;
But green when the comer,
Who brings us the summer,
The cuckoo calls clear o'er the
Westmorland dales.

H D Rawnsley

The only grand things I have seen during the whole summer have been Borrowdale, Wordsworth and York Minster.

W C Macready, 1823

Time was I stood, as thou does now
And viewed the dead as Thou dost me;
Ere long Thou'lt lie as low as I,
And others stand and look on thee.
Headstone at Rosthwaite

It rained nearly all day, and at last, in despair of better weather, we sallied out in waterproofs to look at Rydal Falls: they are not imposing either in height or breadth; the scenery around is beautiful.

Lewis Carroll, 1856

God made men, and men made money;
God made bees, and bees made honey;
But the Devil himself made lawyers
and 'torrneys,
And placed them in U'ston and Dalton
i' Forness.
John Audland of Crosthwaite, 1700s

In this vain world short was my stay
    An' empty was my laughter;
    I go before and lead the way,
    And thou comes jogging after
Epitaph at Wetheral church near Carlisle

Blawith poor people,
An auld church and new steeple,
As poor as hell,
They had to sell
A bit of fell
To buy the bell,
Blawith poor people.
19th century rhyme

There's only two things to do here, make love or go fishing - and t' beck's dried up.

Hotelier to couple during a particular dry spell

Windermere and Keswick are the official gates to the Lake District; in addition there is a sort of tradesman's entrance, the approach from the sea coast via Wastwater, a way that should be reserved for the initiated because it leads so directly to the secret heart of the fells, Scafell itself; and another beautiful side-entrance, very private, is by Ennerdale.

E F Bowman, The English Countryside

I discovered that the Lake Country is a glorious region, of which I had only seen the similitude in dreams, waking or sleeping.
Charlotte Brontë

The Herdwick is a true Lakelander.
take it away from its native fells and
sheep-runs and it refuses to live.
Sydney Moorhouse on the local sheep

T' wedder wain't git warmer till t' snaw's off them hills; an' t' snaw wain't goo off them hills till it gits warmer.

Old Cumbrian weather forecast

Nowt good comes ower t' Raise
Saying from Ambleside and Hawkshead

If they say winter's coming, don't believe them – they said the same thing about summer.

Old Cumbrian weather proverb

With this hive, Ee're all alive,
Good liquor makes us funny.
If you be dry, step in and try
The flavour of our honey.
Former sign outside the Beehive Inn,
Eamont Bridge

If the cuckoo lights on a bare bough,
Keep your hay and sell your cow.
But if he comes on the blooming May,
Keep your cow and sell your hay.
Cumbrian farming forecast

When Skiddaw fell puts on a cap,
Criffel hills begin to drop.
Old weather proverb

Does it always rain?
Naw, it sometimes snaws.
*Response to tourist's query at Seathwaite
Farm (the wettest inhabited house in
England)*

A snowy April and a snizy May,
Maks farmers ettle oot their hay.
Old Cumbrian saying on the weather

There's allus mair room at t' top o' t' stee than there is at t' bottom (the ladder of success).
Old Cumbrian saying

I had saved £5 for a week off. It was the first time I had ever been away from home. I went with a friend to see the Lakes I had heard people talk about. It was the moment that changed my life. I was absolutely captivated. I did not know there was a beauty in the world like I found in the Lake District. I did not want to go back to a treasurer's office on a big town council. All I wanted was to live a quiet life in the Lake District.

Alfred Wainwright on his first visit to the Lakes, aged 23

Shrove Tuesday, Shrove Tuesday, Jack
went to plough,
His mother made pancakes, she
scarcely knew how.
She tossed them, she turned them, she
made them so black
With soot from the chimney that
poisoned poor Jack.
Old Cumbrian rhyme

Westmorland, a country eminent only for being the wildest, most barren and frightful of any that I have passed over in England, or even in Wales itself.

Daniel Defoe, 1724

Mardale Green… lost its life by drowning… all that is left are ghosts.

Alfred Wainwright

When Wansfell wears a cap of cloud
The road of Brathay will be loud;
When mists come down on
Loughrigg fell,
A drenching day grayheads foretell.
The Ambleside Weather Glass, 1870s

Crooked by nature is never made
straight by education.
Cumbrian saying

If it's quite tidy (calm) doon there,
thoo can wesh today.
Weather forecasting using Windermere

When no one at the pier has cried
'This is the bus for Ambleside',
When all of us shall mend our ways,
The sun will shine for seven days!
The Ambleside Weatherglass, 1870s

Haweswater… in the throes of being converted into yet another waterworks for Manchester. Surely the people of Manchester must be the cleanest, within and without, the British Isles.

Doreen Wallace, 1940

When t' gadfly's aboot, t' weather's bad.
Cumbrian farmers' saying

And if you, dear reader, should get a bit of grit in your boot as you are crossing Haystacks in the years to come, please treat it with respect. It might be me.

Alfred Wainwright who wanted his ashes scattered on Haystacks

Hire 'im with 'is britches' knees oot,
not 'is britches' arse.
Saying from farm hiring days

Stanley Ghyll or Dalegarth Force, what matters it? Here is one of the choice places of the earth.

Mrs Linton, 1860s

Devon's fine and Dorset, Cornwall
down afar,
Surrey has her lovers where the roses are.
But my heart's up Northward, my
devotion's given
To the land where mountains kiss the
brow of heaven.

Cumberland Way, Cumberland Way.
Caw Fell and Steeple at dawn of day.
Wild moor and meadow in sunshine
and shadow
That's where my heart is —
Cumberland Way.

Southern girls are pretty, very witty too.
Dainty as the angels, eyes of every hue.
But the girls up Northward, happy are
and free.
Give me one, she'll journey twenty
miles with me.

Cumberland Way, Cumberland Way,
Caw Fell and Steeple at dawn of the day.
On through the heather just two hearts
together.
That's where my dreams are,
Cumberland Way.

Continued...

Long I've left the mountains, long I've
been down here,
But I see my own land oft in vision clear.
Lake and vale and homestead, sun and
rain and snow.
Brave hearts wait there for me, back at
last I'll go.

Cumberland Way, Cumberland Way,
Caw Fell and Steeple at dawn of day.
Soon I'll be roaming, Ah! soon I'll be
homing.
That's where my love is –
Cumberland Way.
Traditional song

Nivver envy a man cos he can ride a car. Maybe he's got rheumatics.
Overheard in Grasmere

It takes a bit of getting used to on paper; it looks very awkward, as if it had forgotten to take off its walking boots and clomped onto the nice clean page too rudely. It demands to be spoken.

Melvyn Bragg on Cumbrian dialect

Gull, gull, fly to the sand
There's always bad weather
When you're on the land.
Weather folklore from Cartmel

The first thing which I remember as an event in my life was being taken by my nurse to the brow of Friar's Crag on Derwentwater.

John Ruskin

A week o' this would do more good in an hour or two than a month of it would in a week.

Lake District labourer during a drought

It is an astonishing piece of England, the greatest surprise and delight that awaits the English traveller who has not been this way. It has deep solitudes, majestic heights, and the solemn beauty of still water, a grouping of natural beauty uncommon in this country and seen here at its best.

Arthur Mee, 1930

Haweswater is a lesser Ullswater, with this advantage, that it remains undefiled by the intrusion of bad taste.
William Wordsworth, 1835

I do not want them to see Helvellyn
when they are drunk.
*John Ruskin's fears about the influx of
lower classes on the arrival of the railway to
the Lakes*

Our Frank's just like a cow tail – he's
allus ahint.
Will Ritson on his son

Keep yer dogs on t' lead. We dooant want fower starters an' six finishers – it upsets t' judges.

Master of ceremonies before the hounds race at a Lakeland show

The tourist who is not in haste to scale some mighty fell will linger long in this Paradise within a Paradise, where he may wander at will. Those who are in a hurry should eschew the place. It is too good for them.

Baddeley on the Rosthwaite area of Borrowdale

When I walked the fells, animals were my only companions. They had an uncomplaining acceptance of the conditions in which they lived – out in dreadful weather all the time.

Alfred Wainwright

You have entered within the gates of one of Nature's grandest temples, and have caused the echo of some of her noblest harmonies.

Mrs Linton on Wasdale, 1860s

No tufted verdue graces its banks, nor hanging woods throw rich reflections on its surface: but every form, which it suggests, is savage and desolate.

William Gilpin on Thirlmere, 1772

I calls yon woman peninsular. A long
neck sticking out to see.
Old Cumbrian farmer's observation

There's nee 'casion lad fer us to cum up to London, cos some o' seets o' London cums doon here to see us.

Will Ritson on being asked to see the sights of the capital

To whichever quarter a bull faces in lying on All-Hallows Eve, from thence the wind will blow the greatest part of the winter.

Old Cumbrian weather forecast

It's like this, lads; God gave us so much ground we had to pile it up i' great big heaps.

Farmer's response to campers who said the site was too steep for tents

A congregation of smells, like Wasdale
Head Chapel in salving time.
Provost Fox on Wasdale

The whole scene is entirely of the horrid kind. Not a tree appeared to add the least cheerfulness to it.

Gilpin on Dunmail Rise, 1772

The highest mountain, the deepest lake
and the biggest liar.
*Auld Will Ritson on Wasdale's claims to
fame (including himself)*

Ah can't see what t' fuss is aboot. It's nobbut staines and watter.
Lakeland farmer's assessment of the scenery

There seem as many ways of fastening
a gate as there are gates… no two are
quite alike.
Alfred Wainwright

T' fog were so thick, if we hedn't known where we were, we wouldn't hev known where we were.

Cumbrian farmer in pub conversation

What's makkin' ye fellas fash yer-sels seea mich aboot climming t' crags? Isn't t' fells big eneugh for ye?

Will Ritson of Wasdale Head (on climbers)

No doubt Wordsworth had too many
women about him, ready to humour
him at any hour by taking up the pen
in his service.
Eric Robertson, 1911

I've one foot in t' grave and t' other on
a banana skin ready for slipping in.
Remark by an old Penruddock man

St Bega's head seen fair and clear,
Is a sign of westerly breezes here.
Old Cumbrian weather forecast

I trace continuously the tacit reference in my Cumberland built soul to moorish Skiddaw and far-sweeping Saddle-back as the proper types of majestic form.

John Ruskin, 1885

Not a single red tile, no gentleman's flaring house or garden walls, break in upon the repose of this little unsuspecting paradise.

Thomas Gray on Grasmere, 1769

Nivver thee wed a woman wid a fortune. My wife hed five pund, an' I nivver heard t' last on't.
Old Cumbrian farmer

Of all the lake country villages,
Grasmere is the most picturesque and
the most like one's ideas of the typical
English home.
E Lynn Linton, 1864

When t' day begins to lengthen,
The cawld begins to strengthen.
Old Cumbrian saying on the weather

Tak brandy externally tul the hair grows, and then tak it internally to clinch t' reeats.
Cumbrian cure for baldness

For my part I have never told a lie in my life.

A former Bishop of Carlisle, visiting Temple Sowerby Lying Contest to tell the villagers how foolish their annual competition was. He won first prize.

Yan-a-dick, tyan-a-dick, tether-a-dick,
methera-a-dick, bumfit, yan-a-bumfit,
tyan-a-bumfit, tether-a-bumfit,
methera-a-bumfit, giggot.
*11-20 in the ancient sheep counting system
used around Borrowdale and Keswick*

If October ice will bear a duck,
At Christmas 't will be sludge and
muck.

Old Cumbrian saying on the weather

Wordsworth was a native of the district, an out-and-out Northerner of largely Scandinavian stock.
Norman Nicholson, 1955

Grasmere is too busy to grow
beautiful.
A Victorian artist

If thoo knows nowt, say nowt; if thoo knows summat, say less.
Old Cumbrian saying

He is stubborn but intensely loyal. He has tenacity and resolution. He has a great gift of silence. There is nobody who dislikes criticism so much. He is conservative in his habits. He is by no means sentimental, but you can go to him with your troubles. He does not express his amazing affection for those who live in his vicinity until he is quite certain that they are safely dead.

Dr Herbert Williams (former Bishop of Carlisle) on the typical Cumbrian

Hungry and thin we staggered in;
Happy and stout we waddled out.
Old Dungeon Ghyll visitors' book

Gee, you must have some mighty fierce
sheep up here.

*American tourist on seeing 'Beware of
Sheep' sign in Patterdale*

...that dale... where Kendale towne
doth stand
for making of our cloth scarce match'd
in all the land.
Michael Drayton, 1622

Silence is always more profound where once there was noise.
Alfred Wainwright commenting on former mining areas of the Lakes

Many a good top-cwoat covers a gay
(very) shabby suit.
Old Cumbrian saying

He was rough in manner and not
attractive to children, and was always
prophesying danger, and had no
sympathy with our desire to climb.
Description of Will Ritson, 1856

He was the Cumberland Statesman to the very marrow of his backbone. An intercourse with almost every class of society extending over two generations of men, had not the slightest perceptible influence in changing either his manners or his dialect.

Baddeley guide on Will Ritson

It has been the capital of Cumbria, it has suffered from the Scottish raiders and seen the Jacobite rebels, it has kept a rather pathetic fragment of a castle, and has some charming peeps of the old world for those who walk to see them.

Arthur Mee on Penrith, 1937

Helvellyn slopes where Coleridge crept
and Southey sprang
Where Wordsworth hoisted up with
ropes
Took out his fountain pen and sang.

Anon

Grasmere was very solemn in the last glimpse of twilight; it calls home the heart to quietness.

Dorothy Wordsworth's Journal, 1800

If yon were nobbut grass, thou could
git a thumping lot o' sheep on it.
*A sheepman from Westmorland commenting
on Morecambe Bay*